Audubon's Sparrow

Advance Praise

"With Audubon's birds perched, like witnesses, in the corner of its and the readers' imaginations, this intimate and moving collection sings a richly woven, whispery tale of their creation. At its center, Lucy Bakewell Audubon and her world of early America come to scrabbling, courageous life, one of sacrifice, mystery, and endurance—of love, in other words. What I find mysterious, to paraphrase a philosopher, is the background against which what I experience has its meaning. Juditha Dowd's elegant and enchanting *Audubon's Sparrow* provides a version of that background for these birds and these lives, against which they sing a newly meaningful song."

—David Daniel, author of *Ornaments*

"In *Audubon's Sparrow*, Juditha Dowd masterfully blends lyric intensity with narrative in a sequence that gives us Lucy Bakewell Audubon not only as the wife of the renowned ornithologist, but also as a compassionate woman of great resourcefulness and courage. Using imagined diary entries and letters, the book moves us from the sweetness of a first love embedded in the natural world ("you have taught me to see / not only the cardinal // but light itself") through the many challenges and resolutions of a life made difficult by poverty and a famous husband's mercurial temperament."

—Pamela Alexander, author of *Commonwealth of Wings: An Ornithological Biography Based on the Life of John James Audubon*

"In Juditha Dowd's *Audubon's Sparrow*, in which Audubon's wife, Lucy Bakewell, recounts her life with the great artist, some poems are airy, light, like little wrens flitting tree to tree, branch to branch; others, more like owls perched there, above the world but of it, their unblinking eyes taking in everything— both equal parts of Lucy's character. More distant, high in the sky and hovering, always hovering, is Audubon himself, that glitzy, powerful, and mercurial raptor of a man and artist casting his large shadow. In Dowd's poetic hands, though, Lucy escapes that shadow, emerging into light. This, and the poetic vitality and variety of form she brings to bear, mark Dowd's high achievement."

—George Drew, author of *Drumming Armageddon*

"These persona poems form a book-length narrative which tells the story of the Audubons' courtship and marriage, their journey west, the many moves, the long years of separation and crossed letters, Audubon's petulance, and Lucy's making a life of her own, on her own. Some take the form of letters, some are tender love poems: 'I am your cello / bowed allegro moderato / I am your wild persimmon sweet and ripe.' Lucy calls Audubon 'Bird-catcher,' 'Dreamer,' 'my errant passerine,' 'husband to his birds.' This is a compelling story, which reads like a novel and wisely leaves the last word to Lucy."

—Barbara Crooker, author of *Some Glad Morning*

AUDUBON'S SPARROW

A Biography-in-Poems

JUDITHA   DOWD

Rose Metal Press

2020

All rights reserved. No part of this book may be used or reproduced in any manner without written permission except in the case of brief quotations within critical articles and reviews. Please direct inquiries to:
Rose Metal Press, Inc.
P.O. Box 1956, Brookline, MA 02446
rosemetalpress@gmail.com
www.rosemetalpress.com

Names: Dowd, Juditha, author.
Title: Audubon's sparrow : a biography-in-poems / Juditha Dowd.
Identifiers: LCCN 2020000064 (print) | LCCN 2020000065 (ebook) | ISBN
    9781941628218 (paperback ; acid-free paper) | ISBN 9781941628225 (ebook)
Subjects: LCSH: Audubon, Lucy Green Bakewell, 1787-1874--Poetry. | Audubon,
    John James, 1785-1851--Poetry. | Ornithologists--United States--Poetry.
    | Artists--United States--Poetry. | LCGFT: Poetry.
Classification: LCC PS3604.O93836 A93 2020 (print) | LCC PS3604.O93836
    (ebook) | DDC 811/.6--dc23
LC record available at https://lccn.loc.gov/2020000064
LC ebook record available at https://lccn.loc.gov/2020000065

Photo and artwork credits, as well as bibliographical material, can be found in the back of the book.

Cover and interior design by Heather Butterfield.

Cover design includes images of "Letter from John J. Audubon to Lucy Audubon," January 1, 1827, Library of Congress, public domain.

This book is manufactured in the United States of America and printed on acid-free paper.

For Mae Smith Eastmond
(1884–1983)

with love and gratitude

Table of Contents

PAPAGENO

TWO WORLDS

EQUIPOISE

Preface

What does it mean to sacrifice for someone else's art? Midway through Richard Rhodes' brilliant biography *John James Audubon: The Making of an American* I kept returning to this question. My interest in the naturalist had shifted toward his wife, Lucy Bakewell. How might she have viewed the arduous early decades that shaped their long relationship, years when she was often unsupported by an absent husband, relying instead on her own wits and courage? My interest soon led me to a fine biography by the late Carolyn E. DeLatte, one of the few works I could find that made Lucy its focus rather than John James. I was curious, too, about the swamp sparrow Audubon included in *The Birds of America*, a watercolor he asked the engraver to inscribe with Lucy's name. Had she drawn the picture herself, or, as some say, was he equating Lucy with a little bird he called "timid, destitute of song," traits opposite those of his tall and spirited wife, an accomplished musician? Perhaps his well-known sense of humor was at play. My guess is he was simply acknowledging his debt to her. For beyond doubt is Lucy's support of his ambition, both emotionally and financially, the latter remarkable at a time when women were barred from outside employment. (Fortunately for the Audubons, teaching was an exception, considered at the time a lowly albeit acceptable domestic occupation.) While it is plain that both Audubons gave up much in pursuit of his dreams, in my estimation she paid the greater price.

A quarter century after the American Revolution, Lucy Bakewell arrived in New York with her wealthy English family. Named for her mother, she was then fifteen years old—bright, curious, capable, and charming, the eldest of six children. DeLatte mentions Lucy's fondness for gardening and that she owned a copy of Erasmus Darwin's two-part book *The Botanic Garden*, a brilliantly quirky blend of poetry, science, and Enlightenment thought that hints broadly at theories later developed by his grandson Charles. Descended from a line of Derbyshire gentry, Lucy's father, William Bakewell, had been involved with the political, religious, and scientific controversies of eighteenth-century England. The Darwin and Priestley families were Bakewell friends. Rhodes notes in his book that, as had been the case for Joseph Priestley, William's dissenting views on certain issues may have compromised his ability to remain safely in his homeland. Whether this was the reason he decided to follow friends and family to the young country with its fresh opportunities, we cannot know for certain. Such a journey was hazardous in an era when one out of six ships crossing the Atlantic was lost at sea. That and other risks of uprooting his young family would have been carefully considered.

William's first business venture was a Connecticut brewery he owned with one of his brothers. Evidently it was not as successful as he'd hoped, and when it burned to the ground he moved his family to a sizeable property northwest of Philadelphia, where he again took up his interest in progressive agriculture. The plantation's isolated location must have seemed rather lonely to the children, who had enjoyed an active social life in Derbyshire surrounded by generations of people they knew well. But within weeks of arriving at their new home, the Bakewells would meet another recent immigrant, the handsome young Frenchman residing at a neighboring farm called Mill Grove.

The illegitimate offspring of Jean Audubon, a bold merchant-ship captain, and a French chambermaid named Jeanne Rabin, Jean Rabin was born in 1785 on his father's sugar plantation in Saint-Domingue (now Haiti). His mother died during his infancy, and he was raised until age six by his father's quadroon housekeeper, who resumed her previous relationship with the captain and bore a daughter. Soon after, with slave revolution imminent, both children were transported to France, formally adopted by the captain and his wife, and their surnames names changed to Audubon in 1794. Jean's first name was also modified to Jean-Jacques at this time. In 1803, seeking to spare his by-now teenage son conscription in Napoleon's army, Captain Audubon secretly shipped him off to the Pennsylvania farm he'd bought earlier as a hedge against losses in Haiti.

Audubon senior's farm at Mill Grove had been managed by a Quaker tenant couple for some time. They made young Audubon welcome and indulged his youthful swagger. In short order Jean-Jacques anglicized his name and began disguising his background with grand tales that he himself may have come to half-believe. Had they known the truth of his awkward ancestry, the Bakewells would probably not have permitted Audubon to court Lucy, despite their Enlightenment views on other matters.

Eventually, in 1808, the couple married and set out for Kentucky, joining the great westward migration of the nineteenth century. Audubon's published works provide vivid scenes of the frontier life they encountered, as travels over the next two decades took them along the Ohio and Mississippi Rivers to New Orleans. While Lucy's words can be found in her surviving letters, we most often glimpse her obliquely, in the shared life as told by others, the spotlight on her flamboyant husband. This is a poet's loss and luxury.

Audubon's Sparrow aims to tell Lucy's story in her voice and from her perspective, but it grew out of an imaginative empathy for both Lucy and John James. And while it is rooted in generally accepted accounts of their life and times, it makes no claims as to precise historical accuracy. Except for a handful of italicized lines taken from her actual letters, Lucy's correspondence and diary entries are my own inventions. She often called her sons by their middle names, Gifford and Woodhouse, but only first names are used here to avoid confusion. Quoting Audubon's work, much of it already heavily edited by others, I take the liberty of nudging his colorful prose into loose poetic form, subtracting but not adding words. I have also included a few dramatic monologues in the "voice" of John James, though not in his actual words, poems that imagine his thoughts at points in Lucy's narrative.

In several places throughout the book I have borrowed the figure of Papageno from Mozart's comic opera *The Magic Flute*. In this allegory of reason and enlightenment, love and loss, Papageno the bird-catcher dresses as a bird himself as he wanders the woods. Boastful, claiming heroic deeds actually performed by others, and yearning for his lady love, Papageno is by turns exotic, mercurial, sympathetic, silly, and wise. This character kept popping into my mind as I read the Rhodes biography, for John James often reminded me of Papageno, an exaggerated version of the naturalist at his best and worst. *The Magic Flute* debuted in 1791 and was by all accounts a success. Lucy's parents may well have attended one of the many performances staged throughout Europe in the decade before they emigrated. And I've imagined Mozart among the composers whose work they regularly enjoyed on musical evenings at Fatland Ford, their Pennsylvania plantation. Papageno's parts are light-hearted and simple, befitting his character. Competent amateur musicians would have been able to play them.

In the end, music may be the hero of Lucy's story. For without its comforts, to say nothing of it becoming her livelihood, Lucy may not have been able to withstand the hardships and loneliness that dogged her for so many years. She might have given up and returned to her relatives, defeated and embittered. Had this been the case, it is my belief that, for all his brilliance, most of us today would never have heard of John James Audubon.

La Forest

"Come and be my little starling."
—Papageno

from *The Magic Flute*, Wolfgang Amadeus Mozart

Monsieur

Diary
January, 1804
Norristown,
Pennsylvania

Today our neighbor at Mill Grove paid us a welcome call.
Belatedly, I add. Had not my father met him Monday
hunting in our woods, would he have come at all?

I sent a servant to the barns to summon Father.
We waited in the parlor, I sewing a shirt for little Will.
With open curiosity *monsieur* surveyed the room,
moved closer to inspect my work, claimed he found
my stitchery *très délicat.*

Bold of him, I thought.

We spoke in both our languages as etiquette required;
it was queer to note his preference for the Quaker *thou.*
His chestnut hair falls well below his shoulder,
and he is quite the dandy.

September, 1804
Fatland Ford,
Norristown,
Pennsylvania

Dearest Cousin Euphemia,

Since Mother took ill I am preoccupied with the children,
helping Ann with penmanship and Sarah with her sums—
leaving little time for riding or the garden.

Mother pines for Derbyshire, but Father is plainly fond
of his new estate. He's changed the name from Vaux Hill
to Fatland Ford. Perhaps he hopes to stimulate the harvest?

A neighbor, Mr. Audubon, has befriended us of late,
here from France to avoid conscription in Napoleon's war.
He lives on the farm his father bought some years ago
when Saint-Domingue slave revolts threatened his plantation.

La Forest, I call our good *monsieur*, from his native *La Forêt*.
Some afternoons we seek the birds he likes to draw.
As to how he pronounces my name, you may not be surprised
to learn I now prefer it uttered by the French.

Light

There,

on the limb of that red-leafed tree…

you have taught me to see
        not only the cardinal

but light itself
                and the wind in it.

Now as I move through Father's fields
the wheat divides

        weighs against my thighs
                like water in a creek

        like a hand might
                if it brushed me

unintentionally.

December, 1805
Fatland Ford

Dearest Cousin,

I am helping Mr. Audubon improve his English,
and he returns the favor by tutoring me in French
(mine being limited and apparently old-fashioned).

If he stays for supper our evenings are improved,
for Mr. A is fond of dancing. He treats us to his fiddle
or accompanies me on pianoforte, and he's taught us all
some charming French *chansons.*

His lively conversation always pleased poor Mother
and entertains my siblings to this day,
yet Father still resists a suitor he deems unsuitable.

Often he reminds me I am but eighteen.

Tomorrow Morning

Diary
April 5, 1808
Fatland Ford

La Forest returned to us on Monday night
along with his new partner Ferdinand Rozier—
both cheerful, and none the worse for wear.
Louisville, they swear, has opportunity!

We will wed in the parlor at half past ten.
At last it is to be.

Madame Audubon

How will they fit in two small chests
these goods I've stitched all year?
The larger must go to towels and quilts
but I need this one for clothes—
3 shifts
a petticoat
collars
summer gloves
the plain muslin nightdress
and this pleated one you say you love

the high-waist gown I've trimmed in Mother's lace
(how I wish she could have lived to see our happiness).

2 cotton dresses
        yes I must have two
my warm wool jacket with embroidery

these boots will do
and oh   my dancing slippers
and the wooden pattens Cousin sent
to protect them from the streets.

                    ***

Headed west this rainy morning
        the track more rock than road
I remember our courtship   *husband*
(again the thrilling word)
how we begged the fathers to permit our marriage

Too young! What prospects?
how you all but drowned four years ago—
a fall through ice on Perkiomen Creek
        and I your nurse till spring

and that phoebe pair you showed me once
lovebirds you called them
        leveling your gaze.

In the mountains before Pittsburgh
I step down to spare the horses
        walk with you in the muddy rut.

           ***

When you pulled me from the battered coach
I barely knew my name
the terror as we overturned
        the horses' screams…

I feared then you would break my bones
        so tight you held me
the way you cried *my wife*

my wife.

March, 1809
Louisville,
Kentucky

Dearest Cousin Euphemia,

At the end of a year we find ourselves still living
at the Indian Queen Hotel—less rough than others
where we've stayed, although every bit as noisy.
Hoping soon to rent a house, retrieve our belongings,
yet pleased to have our own room now
(where no one spits tobacco juice),
as private as we could wish.

Mr. Audubon is busy at his general store
when not off hunting rabbits, or sketching them,
or racing his fine horse. He has an excellent
disposition and a merry heart, adding much
to our nights and days. Already we have made
new friends, the Berthouds and the Tarascons—
so many here are French.

As my confinement nears I pass the time in sewing.
How I long to have a book!

Henderson, Kentucky

Summer, 1810

We loaded up a flatboat to capacity
        floated a hundred miles downstream
                to open the new store.

Less competition here
        more birds to draw.

This sturdy cabin is our first real home
My husband writes in his journal
As better could not be had we were pleased.

With us we brought flour and some bacon hams
The woods he writes *are amply stocked with game.*

He Breaks with Rozier

Diary
April, 1811
Henderson

Finally La Forest has returned from St. Genevieve.
The hundred miles between the ports are difficult
this time of year, the woodlands soft with thaw.
The distance gave him two hard days of walking.

He has dissolved the partnership except for monies owed,
finding the site a poor one for another general store.
I admit I am relieved. Rozier is high-handed.
He wants no truck with any but his fellow French.

Let him keep that store while we continue here.

A Visit to Fatland Ford

December, 1811

Is it wise   I asked him twice   to travel so close to winter
but he was unconcerned
we had our health and the excellent horses.

Our Victor   so young but eager
sat before his Papa on the big-shouldered bay
which (besides the boy) is his father's pride.

From Louisville to Pittsburgh
I write now to Euphemia
the chief part is through woods where the Sun scarcely penetrates.

We forded the Ohio in a snow squall
memory of our westbound trek three years ago still fresh.
The roads most dreadful at all seasons...

Leaving the foothills we scanned the plain ahead
and finally my father   dry clothes
an ample bed.

Now the difficulties and fatigue are over I can scarcely realize
that I have rode on horseback nearly eight hundred miles.

Another Opportunity

Diary
January, 1812
Fatland Ford

La Forest and my brother Tom have determined to be partners—
AUDUBON & BAKEWELL—we like the sound of it—
New Orleans factors for a Liverpool establishment.

New Orleans? Exotic, I suppose, the weather mild.
Too cold here now to hunt. My husband spends his hours
mounting specimens and drawing.

I will prepare to move again.

PLATE XCI.

Broad-winged Hawk.

FALCO PENNSYLVANICUS, &c.

Male 1 Female 2

Broad-winged Hawk

(*Falco pennsylvanicus, Wils.*)
from Ornithological Biography *by John James Audubon*

I put the bird on a stick made fast to my table [. . .]
Its eye, directed towards mine, appeared truly sorrowful,
with a degree of pensiveness that rendered me quite uneasy.

I measured the length of its bill with a compass,
began my outlines, continued measuring part after part as I went on,
and finished the drawing, without the bird ever moving once.

My wife sat at my side, reading to me at intervals.

War?

Diary
March, 1812
Fatland Ford

Rumor has again delayed our plans.
We should wait here for more definite news
but Father's wife Rebecca makes clear we are a burden.

Reports have reached us of more earthquakes at New Madrid,
the Mississippi River flowing backward!
Our earth is thin-skinned (like some of us)—
I've even felt it tremble here at Fatland Ford.

Father is not himself of late, addled and quite slow.
Eliza has a blindness that I'm treating with poultices.
Only Will is merry, soon to be a man.
Our Victor is enchanted.

Rivers

"He made a spelling of the soft pet of the ivory-billed woodpecker. He told himself always: remember."

—Eudora Welty, "A Still Moment"

Home, 1813

I did not think this kindly once of Henderson
this rough and thinly-populated town
      its river banks the recent haunt of pirates,

but now that our fear of trade blockade is realized
far better we be here than in New Orleans.

Yes   the town is lovely with its prospect of the river
         talk of new prosperity in the air

our old friends the Rankins here to welcome us
and brother Tom as partner in the store.

Yes   at last   a fine log cabin of our own
I'll buy oil lamps for the tables
send for Mother's silver and books to fill the shelves,

the new slave will help me plant the garden.

Unpacking crates of blankets
bathing our little John
     my hope rewarded

        in truth   revived.

Almost Morning

Again I wake to your heat
　　　　your scent of wood smoke

your body　　as familiar as my own
　　　　and yet a mystery...

touch me　　　　yes
　　　　　　　　　　and here

I am your cello
　　　　bowed　allegro moderato

I am your wild persimmon sweet and ripe.

August, 1815
Henderson

Dear Father,

Since Eliza joined our household I have fine company.
She claims young Victor now resembles you.
Has she mentioned she is courted by Nicholas Berthoud?
A young man with potential, well-known to us.

Mr. Audubon has written to your old friend David Prentice
requesting help to build a steam mill here.
Perhaps you'd be kind enough to put in a good word.

Tom talks of opening a second general store,
looks forward to Will's arrival for his apprenticeship.
A Mr. & Mrs. Pears are visiting with their children
while they consider investment in our mill.

And the heat continues, the worst we've yet seen.
We leave doors and windows open to capture any breeze,
till Mr. A's pet turkey wanders in...

We prosper, Father.

Daughter

Lucy   my husband christened her
                to honor me—
Now her suffering binds us more than common name.

Dr. Rankin calls the problem "water on the brain"
           a disfiguring affliction.

She is fretful at all hours
               always in some pain—

We have no cure says Dr. Rankin.

PLATE CXLII

American Sparrow-Hawk. FALCO SPARVERIUS, *Linn.* Male 1. Female 2. *Butter-nut or Walnut-leaf Juglans cinerea.*

Nero

Screeching in the tulip tree
       this birdy fiddle

this sparrow hawk who argues
the necessity of sparrows.

All spring I caught the little birds
       to provide our hatchling
watched La Forest rend them
       so Nero could eat.

Nero   our Nero
terrifying the chickens
and the wood ducks in our pond

soon to have no need of us
       sufficient
yet here he stays
orphan   outcast
       separate from his kind

a creature like my husband
part this   part that

yet neither one   reliably.

Audubon, at the Window

I do not dissemble when I say that I'm a happy man,
   though something weak within me says I'm not.
      Fall has unmistakably arrayed our woods,
and ice has skimmed the creek beyond that stand of holly.
   I cannot see it, for I'm here amid the bales and boxes,
      flour bins and raisins, and the woolen socks,
      hoes and skillets, twine and carriage straps,
      the cabinet where we keep the guns and shot.

I'm a provisioner of farmers, of travelers and families,
      while something in me sighs that I am not.

My Husband Does Not Lie

Tom is mistaken
        confused by his discouragement...

If only he could see La Forest
        coming in at dawn

his soaking feet and bloody shirt
a bag of quail for breakfast.

It is ardor   it is hope
not laziness but too much life—
a man like this is not a clerk by nature.

I fear he cannot learn it.

See him with his charcoal
and his colored chalks
        bending over paper late at night

another candle we can ill afford.

Passenger Pigeon

(Columba migratour, Linn.)
from Ornithological Biography by *John James Audubon*

The Pigeons, arriving by the thousands,
alighted everywhere, one above another.
Here and there perches gave way with a crash,
and, falling to the ground, destroyed hundreds
of the birds beneath [. . .]

The howling of wolves now reached our ears [. . .]

The pigeons were picked up and piled in heaps,
until each had as many as he could possibly dispose of,
when the hogs were let loose to feed on the remainder.

Before the Boys Awoke

we took our horses through the woods—
with our Lucy gone we seek relief from sorrow.

I gave my all   arriving first
            turned round to tease him
till he pulled me laughing from my saddle—

ten years
            yet sometimes still a bride.

We rode the way we came
neck and neck
            my hair undone
                        and streaming out behind

the trees alive   the sun already rising.

Ruin

Diary
February, 1819
Henderson

The Louisiana Debt is due and must be paid in specie.
All the banks have called their loans,
chasing panic through the Territory.

We are loath to sell our land at sacrifice,
yet even this will not suffice to save the stores or mill.
Partners want repayment, we have but half the price.

Our little daughter, and now our livelihood.
What else, I wonder, can be torn from us?

Overheard this morning: *Audubon is a braggart,*
Lucy puts on airs.

I Remind Myself about Gossip

For his errors   his exuberance   we find ourselves
discredited among people once called friends—

shiftless they name him   behind my back
while he is gone to look for work.

What wife escapes a husband's reputation?

Partial Bill of Sale

John James & Lucy Bakewell Audubon to
Nicholas & Eliza Bakewell Berthoud,
Henderson, Kentucky, 1819

1. Two general stores, complete with unsold goods
2. Half-interest in a Prentice steam mill

I listen as he blames himself
and try not to agree—

too trusting   no head for business—

but times are bad all over
four neighbors gone
others   like ourselves   in bankruptcy.

***

6. Double log house and contents
8. Musical instruments, including one pianoforte

My sons yawn beside the hearth
I stir their porridge

recall bright nights of fiddle and flute
of dancing by the fire

and overhead the darting parakeets.

***

13. twelve tracts of wooded land
23. … and three dozen silver spoons

It's not so much the land
for someday there will be more

or the oval mirrors   our Windsor chairs
the linens I have folded into cedar-scented drawers—

family things that Father passed to me
his eldest girl.

It's only that my thumbs will miss
what I've always cleaned myself
the ivory hilts that have to be kept from water

and those delicate few with scallop-shell bowls
Mother reserved for turtle soup.

***

35. personal effects … excepting his original drawings
and one gun

and the clothes we wear this damp spring morning,
a few belongings returned to us by brother-in-law Berthoud
who bought them all to protect us from the creditors…

and my books so I may teach our sons…

and my sorrel horse and saddle.

May, 1820
Louisville

Dearest Cousin Euphemia,

In a year of constant troubles we feel most the loss
of our infant, Rose. Her father drew her likeness
as she lay with fever, but even then she seemed to me
a ghost.

I write you from our new address in Louisville.
My husband is making portraits, popular here in town.
Soon we'll move upriver. There he's promised work
at the new Western Museum.

September, 1820
Cincinnati, Ohio

Dearest Cousin Euphemia,

Mr. Audubon's birds are the talk of Cincinnati!
Dr. Drake, director of the new Western Museum,
compares them favorably to Alexander Wilson's.

I am tutoring a few students in our little home,
lessons in arithmetic and natural history.
The boys are glad to have companions.

My husband too has students, though he likes but one—
a Joseph Mason—just thirteen, but talented and eager.
He's hired Joseph to paint backgrounds for the birds,
now quite a flock.

We're told the pictures can be published if the collection
is increased, so the two of them will soon head south,
travel the Mississippi to New Orleans.

We have no family here but judge it best
the boys and I remain.

This Afternoon We Saw Them Off

young John waving from the wharf
      as if his arm would break

and Victor stoic.

Eight months we are to manage.
I must collect the monies owed him
for his work at the museum—

we have yet to see a cent of it.

Audubon's Journal: Mississippi River

from Trip to New Orleans in 1820–21 *by John James Audubon*

December 5, 1820

Skinning the catfish was the first job this morning—
done by cutting through the skin in narrow long strips
and tearing these off with a strong pair of pincers.

While at this saw several hundred of these black birds
yet unknown to me that I denominate Black Pelicans,
flying south forming a very obtuse angle
without uttering any noise.

Dr. Drake Hopes to Give Us Something Soon

Diary
December, 1820
Cincinnati

We are owed $1200, enough to keep us for a year.
It seems likely we will realize only part. The Panic
caused such hardship here that patrons have withdrawn,
and Dr. Drake must sell his lovely house.

I do not like to hound the man but we must eat.
Where can I find more pupils?

Audubon's Journal: Mississippi River

from Trip to New Orleans in 1820–21 *by John James Audubon*

December 13, 1820

*About one mile below the mouth of the Arkansas in a thick patch of cane
are two women, the remainder of a party of wandering vagabonds
that about 2 years ago left some part of the eastern state
to proceed to the Promised land—these two wretches
never wash, comb or scarcely clad themselves,
and subsist from the scant generosity of the neighbors,
now and then doing a little sewing.*

Inventory

a pound of meal
a duck egg
a pint of cow's milk

fire in the grate
no wood for tomorrow.

Father Never Treated Me

Diary
December, 1820

as being of a weaker sex, allowing me into his laboratory,
the company of his friends. Our physician, Erasmus Darwin,
much missed since we left England. And Joseph Priestley, too,
who sold us that tract in Pennsylvania, in what he hoped would
one day be a colony (though I think it never came to pass).

I a girl—the eldest—given range of his library,
entrusted with his confidence, proud to manage for him
when dear Mother died...

How could I have known how critical this would be?
How else, in honesty, could I tout myself as tutor now?

But we've lost him to Rebecca.
Oh, Father...

And soon she will lose him to his mind's slow ruin.

Winter

Windows rattle   poorly sealed

      gusts off the Ohio

and nothing left to sell.

Cold   we've known it
who has not

and hunger
not mine so much as theirs
      though mine as well.

But fear…

Papageno

"To tell you all in simple words:
I make my living catching birds."

"What a pleasure it will be
when the gods remember us."

—*The Magic Flute,*
    Wolfgang Amadeus Mozart

Audubon, Distracted

New Orleans

Another urgent letter from my wife.
No funds to send her.
Again no word from either son.
It has dawned only gradually how I've failed them,
that I must call it that.

Here in my portfolio: the woodpecker in flight.
And over there—pinned to a board—
the same bird, lifeless.

Today I'll seek new students
as I must
and advertise for portraits in the marketplace.

But look, this wing,
the position not quite right.
It wants more contrast...

a cleaner white.

PLATE CXII

Downy Woodpecker
PICUS PUBESCENS,
Male & Female. ?
Bignonia capreolata

Drawn from Nature by J. J. Audubon, F.R.S. F.L.S.

Engraved, Printed & Coloured by R. Havell, London, 1831.

I Put Aside Pride

Diary
January, 1821

Today three hundred dollars from La Forest
together with a lovely set of Queen's Ware.

I will leave it crated for we have no shelves.

Eliza has insisted that we go to her,
stay until it's warm enough to safely travel south.

If we depart on Monday I can pay the past-due rent
and have enough left over for our passage.

Fair Incognito

Diary
February, 1821

Dear girl, he writes,
how much I wish to press thee to My Bosom.
I have received a good pair of suspenders,
but thou does not say that they are from thy hands.

And yet he speaks at length of a beautiful Creole,
her nude portrait he has painted over many days.
She pays him with a gun and a kiss
but will not let him visit to review his finished work.

Fair incognito, a wealthy roué's mistress...
this jokester's way of teasing and rewarding a new friend?
I could not reconcile the feelings necessary to draw,
without mingling some of a very different Nature.

A man may well admire a graceful female form,
I find no argument with that—
but might he not remember too the feelings of a wife?
The water in our washbowl—my only looking glass—
is ice tonight. And no one paints my portrait for a kiss.

Dear girl, he writes, *how much I wish.*

A Difficult Balance

Daily I'm reminded of how little we have to keep us,

at first I tried to shield him
        that impulse was mistaken.

How tiresome I sound   even to my own two ears!

Our future lies in following his heart's delight
         it seems our only course

yet we are second now or worse   his sons and I
        all promises delayed.

We march behind the beavers and the shrikes
and even New Orleans' belles
        who one would think from all reports
            pursue him day and night.

Dreamer...
Bird-catcher...   my boastful Papageno

and still he cannot bear an hour's doubt—
it sends him into such despair that all work ceases.

Sister Says We Are Orphans

Diary
March, 1821

Word received this morning from Rebecca—
as usual lacking any warmth.
Father is gone.
No children but Ann for comfort,
though he would not have known us if we came.

Mother adored La Forest for his gaiety.
How she'd laugh and roll her eyes—*The French*!
What I loved, too.
And do.

Yet father was uneasy—he made no bones of it—
stressing the importance of more serious occupations
than tooting flutes and chasing birds.

I am the foolish girl he tried to warn me of.

Audubon's Journal: Mississippi River

from Trip to New Orleans 1820–21 *by John James Audubon*

October 27, 1821

Dressed all new, hair cut, my appearance altered beyond
my expectations, fully as much as a handsome Bird is
when robbed of all its feathering,
and is either entirely neglected or looked upon with contempt;
such was my situation last week—

but when the Bird is well fed, taken care of [. . .]
he is cherished again, nay admired—
such my situation this day—Good God that 40 dollars
should thus be enough to make a Gentleman—
ah My Beloved Country.

.

Doubt

When I've almost thought
        no   decided   we must part

I see again our Lucy
        those long nights back in Henderson

how your hand supported the child's poor head
        your patience with her endless crying.

In the glow of dying fires I saw you wept as well
        soundless
your back bent hard against the dark

        the lit cave it made for the two of you.

Reunion

Diary
December, 1821
New Orleans

As soon as we arrived last night he opened his portfolio,
so many new birds and mammals spread across the floor.

A wonderment overtook me, the mastery he has gained!

Something new inhabits the eyes.
They *see* us.

A Visit from Matabon

Diary
January, 1822
New Orleans

A second *monsieur* in our little house,
he and La Forest jabbering in their native French
and Matabon's instrument a grace note to familiar song.
He even played us snippets from *The Magic Flute*,
that opera Mother loved—
she'd heard it with Father on a visit to Vienna.
I was reminded of our evenings back at Fatland Ford
and our best nights, too, in Henderson...
Oh, the diversions of those happy hours!

For weeks Matabon entertained us, a fine musician—
but he, too, has fallen on hard times.
(La Forest claimed that, when he chanced upon him
in the marketplace, he hardly recognized the man.)
Alone again, we two must face our penury.
Daily La Forest denigrates his art,
says he will destroy it, begin the work anew.

I buy bread and cheese,
as he has no heart to hunt.

May, 1822
New Orleans

Dear Cousin Euphemia,

Your letter much relieves me—
two years without your friendly word
a source, I must admit, of grief.

I am living now with a Mr. & Mrs. Brand,
serving as her tutor and companion,
while my husband has gone to Natchez
where he'd hoped to join a Pacific expedition,
now indefinitely postponed.

Our sons have joined him, but I must stay.
Anne Brand will need me for the birth.

She's a frail girl. I fear for her.

Though I've Little in the Way of Faith, I Pray

Anne's newborn daughter gone by noon.

We lie together in her room
        the unnamed babe between us

           her hair a reddish wisp
    her fingers curled.

My heart reminds me of my own lost girls
but Anne's grief   newly-suffered
that much keener.

I will sit with her all night.

At Beech Woods Plantation, a School

Diary
February, 1823
West Feliciana,
Louisiana

Our friend Dr. Provan has found me this position
with a salary and a cottage, adequate for our needs.
The four of us together once again.

Mistress of the plantation is a widow, Mrs. Percy.
I teach music, writing, and comportment to her girls
and maybe soon to neighbor girls as well.

This seems just now a stroke of luck.

The Feliciana countryside reminds me much
of Derbyshire, its hills and brooks, its gentle green.

How fondly I recall those tender years.

A Most Difficult Day

Diary
July, 1823
Beech Woods

Again La Forest quarrels with Jane Percy,
this time over portraits of her daughters—
their skin too yellow for her preference
though his take is as accurate as he claims.

He spoke harshly, refused to please her
and she has ordered him away.
Of course, he is enraged that I remain—
though I *am* loyal,
rash as he may sometimes be
and was today.

What is the alternative?
We have no other means.

Worse

Midnight
        when he came creeping back

to ask forgiveness
to urge me come away—

Oh   as sorry a sight as I have ever seen.

When at last to bed   friendship restored
        and knowing he must leave by dawn

then our door flung open by a slave
        and Mrs. Percy raving in the torchlight!

By now he's walked the fifteen miles to Bayou Sara
I cannot guess how he will bear this new humiliation

nor how shall I…

Swamp Sparrow.
FRINGILLA PALUSTRIS. Wils.
Male.
May-apple. Podophyllum peltatum.

Drawn from Nature by Lucy Audubon.

Engraved, Printed & Coloured by R. Havell.

On Receiving Dr. Provan's Message

Diary
August, 1823
Natchez

I came by gig in a terrible rush,
a trip that took but half the night
as I did not spare the horse.

Victor and his father hot with fever,
calling out my name.

I feared so we would lose them.

Today they've turned a corner
but recovery may be weeks.

John arrives by coach tomorrow.

A Surprise

yet   not entirely unexpected,
this letter from Jane Percy
            her crisp white page—
will I return?

I fear we must,
            no other plan in sight.

If only she had   if only she might write
I'm sorry...

Our mistress says instead that we're forgiven

            forgiven

and now she'd welcome back
my husband too

a man she's shamed twice over

            and may again.

Audubon's Journal:
A Visit to Mill Grove

from The Life of John James Audubon,
the Naturalist *by Lucy Green Bakewell Audubon*

July 26, 1824

*I abruptly took my hat and ran wildly toward the woods,
to the grotto where I first heard from my wife
the acknowledgment that she was not indifferent to me [...]
It had been torn down, and some stones carted away;
but raising my eyes toward heaven, I repeated the promise
we had mutually made.*

*I returned full of delight. Gave Mr. Haines my portrait,
drawn by myself, on condition that he should have it copied
in the case of my death, and send it to my wife.*

December, 1824
Beech Woods

Dearest Sister Eliza,

Mr. Audubon is to preside here at a cotillion,
teach dancing to our neighbors and their friends.
In truth this year has been among our best.

Be happy for us, Sister. Once more we sing.
His face is not less handsome than the year we met.
Remember? I, a girl, he scarcely older?
Yet somehow we seem younger now.

Again we walk and ride, talking of his travels—
the trip he took to Norristown to visit old Mill Grove,
another to Buffalo, where the wondrous falls so awed him
he refused to paint the scene. Said it would be sacrilege.

And finally it is settled, publication *our* ambition.
He's had no luck pursuing this in Philadelphia;
we hear that Wilson's publisher objected to the competition.
It's Europe then—more interest there in the natural world,
more skill for the engraving.

Last night we paged through all the birds, some I had
quite forgotten. How eager he is to test their fate!
He sails as soon as we have saved enough.

Two Worlds

"[. . .]we are capable of thinking about immortality. That is what sets us apart."

—Cees Nooteboom, "The Following Story"

Audubon's Journal: Dolphins

(aboard the Delos *enroute to England, 1826)*
from Audubon and His Journals
by Maria R. Audubon, quoting John James

How much I have gazed at these beautiful creatures,
watching their last moments of life, as they changed
their hue in twenty varieties of richest arrangement of tints,
from burnished gold to silver bright,
mixed with touches of ultramarine, rose, green, royal purple,
quivering to death on our hard, broiling deck.

[. . .] I longed to restore them to their native element [. . .]
and yet I felt but a few moments before a peculiar sense
of pleasure in catching them with a hook.

.

Mail

Diary
October, 1826
Beech Woods

Finally two letters from La Forest,
safely *there* in England,
displaying his pictures to anyone who asks.
He's lately been adopted by the Rathbones—
prominent, he says, in Liverpool society.

Also word from Victor,
happy at his apprenticeship upriver.
So good with figures, my steadfast boy.

I'm rightly proud.

PLATE XXI

Mocking Bird. TURDUS POLYGLOTTUS, *Linn. Males.1 Females. 2. Florida Jasminum Gelseminum nitidum.*

Mocking Bird

(*Turdus polyglottus, Linn.*)
from Ornithological Biography *by John James Audubon*

The musical powers of this bird have often been taken notice of
by European naturalists [. . .] who find pleasure in listening
to the song of different birds whilst in confinement or at large.
Some [. . .] have described the notes of the Nightingale
as occasionally fully equal to those of our bird.

I [. . .] have no hesitation in pronouncing the notes
of the European Philomel
equal to those of a soubrette *of taste, which, could she study*
under a Mozart might [. . .] become very interesting [. . .]
But to compare her essays to the finished talent of the Mocking Bird,
is in my opinion, quite absurd.

At Dawn Outside My Window

in its pretty cage, our mocking bird—
          its wings spread wide to show the white
              in patches underneath,

its song by turns is plaintive, then vivacious,
and just now a little question in the trills—

this is the bird I've heard all night.

Does it tease me with its changing tunes
or is the thing (as I am) too confined
          and too confused

to have one of its own?

Perhaps we both are pining for a world
          that's slipped away from us

or for a mate that's flown.

November, 1826
Beech Woods

My Beloved Victor,

I'm eager to depart here, son, on account,
as well you know, of the Widow Percy.

We owe much to our friend Nathaniel Pope
(who clerked for us in Louisville—remember?
and now lives near, a well-respected doctor).
He has found me a decent new position.

Beech Grove is smaller than Beech Woods,
but prosperous I'm told. The owner, Mr. Johnson,
has offered to collect the girls' tuitions for me—
not, as I've complained before, a minor thing.

Audubon's Journal: Edinburgh

from Audubon and His Journals
by Maria R. Audubon, quoting John James

November, 1826

*It was settled by Mr. Lizars that he would undertake publication
of the first number of the "Birds of America," and that was enough
to put all my powers of thinking and acting at fever heat. The papers
also began to be more eulogistic of the merits of myself
and my productions, and I felt bewildered with alternate uncertainties
of hope and fear.*

April, 1827
Beech Grove

Dearest Eliza,

You ask after Mr. Audubon.
Last week, a letter written months ago.
Every day he tries to sell subscriptions for his book,
traveling many miles by foot and carriage.

I pray he has trimmed his dangling locks,
so in London and in Edinburgh he is received
respectfully by those who may be of help.

He is husband to his birds now,
and I am... I am what?

Here, I teach my students how to swim,
this body rinsed and for a moment held.

I have almost worn out the piano.

Audubon, Abroad

Teaching in Louisiana, my wife grows weary.
What wife would not?

But I will not give it up, I can't,
though finishing the copper plates
might well mean ten more years abroad,
away from her, away from my America.

Any fool can petition the gods to spare him
from obsession. Any true god will refuse.

The birds. I've forgotten how I came to them,
or did they seek me out instead, a bastard,
born of my father's appetite.

Relentlessly they drive me, like an old horse.
Harried, wild-maned, I take the bit and bridle.

Audubon's Journal:
Liverpool and Manchester

from Audubon and His Journals
by Maria R. Audubon, quoting John James

December 28, 1827

Immediately after breakfast the box came containing the fifth number,
and three full sets for my new subscribers here.
The work pleased me quite.

December 29, 1827

This morning I walked to "Lady" Rathbone's with my fifth number.
It is quite impossible to approach Green Bank,
when the weather is at all fair
without enjoying the song of some birds; for, Lucy,
that sweet place is sacred,
and all the feathered tribe in perfect safety.
A Redwing particularly delighted me today;
I found something of the note of our famous Mock-bird in his melody.

January 1, 1828

Now, my Lucy, when I wished thee a happy New Year this morning
I emptied my snuff box [. . .] and will take no more [. . .]
it is a useless and not very clean habit,
besides being an expensive one. Snuff! farewell to thee.

Boon Companions

Diary
March, 1828
Beech Grove

The Johnsons' guests have just returned from Austria,
their voyage much beset by storms. Both of them are yet
a little weakened.

He's a violinist, while she is quite accomplished on the flute.
She's brought two sheaves of music and some lovely gowns,
as well as this device they call a metronome—a clever thing
for counting time!

To please their hosts the two have planned a musicale,
invited me to join them. Our first piece is a rondo by
L. Beethoven—difficult, but I'm already fond of it.

We practice Sunday afternoons in Mr. Johnson's library.
I hope by May to have my parts learned well enough.

Letters

5 December, 1827
My dearest Lucy,

I had the blues with a vengeance,
I am sorry, quite sorry, dear wife [. . .]
I have wished for thee every moment, and yet [. . .]

I have postponed daily because of what thou *callest*
prudence to write for thee to come.

15 June, 1828
My dear Victor,

I am quite at a loss to grasp anything your Papa writes.
He complains of your silence, says it will be long before
he has finished with the Birds [. . .]

that England is not what it was [. . .]
that I might not like it [. . .]

What he really means I cannot tell—those are his words
and we must interpret them as we can.

Without the Company of My Sons

Diary
October, 1828

When I hear from brother Will how John is thriving
at the academy, I know this choice was right.
His father will be angry that he has no time to draw,
but education cannot wait for our prosperity.

Will—so generous—advancing funds.
When has he disappointed?

No owlets stuffed in pockets now, no muddy feet.
Instead my well-scrubbed girls who study music.

Audubon's Journal: France

from Audubon and His Journals
by Maria R. Audubon, quoting John James

October 13, 1828

At twelve o'clock I was seated in the antechamber of the Vicomte [. . .]
The size of my work astonished him, as it does every one who sees it
for the first time [. . .]

He told me that the work had been under discussion,
and that he advised me to see [. . .] Baron Vacher, the secretary
of the Dauphin [. . .] He gave the signal for my departure by bowing,

and I lifted my book, as if it made of feathers.

Little Ellen Johnson

Diary
November, 1828

cannot be kept from the older girls,
dashing into my classroom when the servants are distracted,
hiding in my skirts.

The child intrigues me. I try to find a task appropriate
to her tender age.

Long ago I lost the hope that life might grant me daughters,
yet here they are.

My Affections?

Diary
November, 1828

Two letters—identical, to guard against sporadic mails.

I cannot but wonder what has happened to his mind.
Do not come to London, he advises
unless willing to accept the *moderate* mode of life
he is prepared to offer.

Pray, do not arrive with a head full of airs!

If you come, he says, not *when*.
If he is still chief in my affections.

He claims I have no thought for him
that I must leave for England *straight away*
or else we had better separate.
Formally, he means to say.

Was it mention of my present situation,
comfortable as it is, that so distressed him?

Or my request he send me two light summer gowns,
as both I have are sadly worn (and out of style),
no hours free to sew my own?

Against better judgment I write of this to Victor,
for often now he seems the firmer friend.

I Will Not Write Tonight

What long ago he freed in me
    or I myself laid open
        to his rootlessness
must close—

        too little range
    in the page's ink
bird feet mocking language.

What of his sons in Louisville
        dependent on my relatives
their lack beyond what I have taught
      or can
their want of a father's hand?

Their want   the way each resembles him
    in trying not to.

I am learning to love the chaste
this book   my room

and outside   a buzzing blackness
where even the moonlit cedars
drown in living water.

          ***

I will not write today...

his demand that I not mention money

(so he may show my letters to his friends
without embarrassment)
offends.

So   I keep my counsel

let him swagger
let him have his bright success

and let it keep accounts for him
        and share his bed.

                    ***

I put away my pen and ink at four
my pupils heading home to their plantations

his latest letter left unread
        perhaps   tomorrow.

Gloves for Victor   vest for John
I will finish them on Sunday
send the gifts upriver with the morning mail.

The stableman will saddle up the chestnut mare
        and I'll ride to Bayou Sara
                buy myself a bonnet

and some dark blue thread.

                    ***

I try again this page begun at dawn

describe a wife you have not seen
                in going on three years

my constitution strong
my black hair turning gray
my gray eyes dimmer

I have lost all my teeth now...

You've been the toast of Edinburgh
          London   Paris too
success we dreamed together
yet somehow

                unexpected...

Come for me   I write.

Equipoise

"Let joyous love for grief atone;
We live by love, by love alone."

—*The Magic Flute*, Wolfgang Amadeus Mozart

Audubon's Journal: France

from Audubon and His Journals
by Maria R. Audubon, quoting John James

December 23, 1828

*Painting every day, and I may well add constantly,
has been the main occupation. I have (what I call)
finished my pictures of the Eagle and the Lamb,
and the Dog and the Pheasants, and now, as usual,
can scarce bear to look at either.*

He Has Another Fit of Blues

Diary
February, 1829
Beech Grove

A letter from La Forest posted August 5—
where it has been these many months I cannot guess.

He claims he must not write to me as a "man in love,"
speaks again to blame me for my failure to be in England.

Who knows what can have prompted it—our letters cross.

While here is peace, the first in years,
my school with fifteen music scholars and a waiting list,

the life I've made.

A New Season

My good horse

the forest's long unbroken line
                    its curling edge of yellow air

and ground birds nesting over there
                watchful

though I have no chalk   no gun
                no snare but curiosity.

It's cooler among the trees.
I'll dismount and take my time
                my ease

                as may any woman left
          to her own care and devices.

Sunlight sparks the trees
          their needles on the wind—

let it   suffice.

Letter from Audubon

6 May, 1829—New York, New York

My dearest friend,

I simply wish to inform thee of my safe arrival here yesterday [. . .]
I have come for thee, dearest Lucy.

Arrived

Diary
June, 1829

Yes, but when am I to see his face?

First he's to the piney woods, the seacoast.
Thou knowest I must draw hard from Nature
every day that I am in America.
Detained now in New York by matters at the Lyceum,
and soon to Philadelphia—where he'll pause
for me to join him. Come! Hurry!

How can he not understand my situation—
completing the lessons, collecting late tuitions,
money we have need of more than ever now...

And skins and plants he demands I gather—
whole trunks-full he'll require for his future work,
and for his friends in England and in France,
who'd fancy a bit of wildlife from the Bayou.

He must not try to send a son to help me.
Let him come himself.

Audubon's Journal: Beech Grove

from Audubon and His Journals
by Maria R. Audubon, quoting John James

November, 1829

The first glimpse of dawn set me on my road,
at six o'clock I was at Mr. Johnson's house;
a servant took the horse,

I went at once to my wife's apartment; her door was ajar,
already she was dressed and sitting by her piano,
on which a young lady was playing.

I pronounced her name.

Squeaky Door

...that nuisance hinge the servant boy neglects to oil and—

Oh!

      turning from little Ellen
   rising from this chair...

the door
      your woolen cap   your stare...

slowly
      my hand on Ellen's shoulder

then quickly as a dream dissolves, I'm moving toward
the words your mouth is making—

      the tumbling *thee* and *thou* and *thine*—

      I who only half-believe

you're here.

Tonight

You　　my fine,
　　　　　　　my was　　and would be,

my errant passerine,

here　　how long
　　　　　　　but here—

your victories unfurled like banners,
　　　　　　　your news and stories shared with all

　　　　　　　and praised by all alike—

this day was yours alone, but for my pride in it.

And here　　　　at last together in my room

　　　　and lovers still,

　　　　　　or once again...

We　　we queer unfeathered breed,

　　　　who are we now, my dear familiar?

Preparing to Leave Beech Grove

Diary
December, 1829

These days fly past with much left to accomplish.
As if possessed, La Forest roams the woods and swamp,
and his freshened sense of purpose is a welcome thing.
However much the man was driven in the past, it is small
compared to how he's now compelled. The book...
the book is everything, is *all*. His boasts are those of one
who knows he finally has a right to them.

A few weeks longer and we're on our way, traveling
upriver for a visit with our sons before we sail to England.
How will I view that far-off land that once was home?
How will we be received?

I've long believed I should be glad to put aside my work,
as heaven knows it has been chiefly toil and duty.
Still, I linger with my pupils when our days are through,
engaged by the music of their chatter, the charm and pleasure
of their beauty. I will leave each one with something
in particular to practice, not too difficult or slight, a piece
to polish on her own till someone new arrives to guide her.

I hope they all will strive to be their own instructors,
for a girl's education seems anything but certain here.

Afterword

The Audubons' reunion was a happy one, perhaps especially so because John James had come to Louisiana rather than continue to insist Lucy travel north to meet him. This fact alone may have rebalanced their by-now shaky relationship, although I suspect they had some frank discussions about the future. Within months they boarded a ship bound for Liverpool. There Lucy joined the ongoing effort to bring her husband's great work, *The Birds of America*, to fruition. It must have been gratifying to see that his talents were admired in her homeland and that his work had a devoted following that might prove to be a steady source of income. According to DeLatte's biography, together they dealt with publishing details, traveled to solicit new subscribers, and met with prominent people who might have ignored them only a few years earlier. When they returned to America in 1831, their sons became part of the family enterprise—Victor as business manager, John collecting and drawing specimens.

Both Audubon sons wed daughters of longtime family friends, the Bachmans. Unfortunately, the marriages were short-lived. When John's wife died of tuberculosis in 1840, Lucy assumed care of his two infant girls. The following year Victor's wife, still childless, succumbed to the same disease that claimed her sister. Sad but determined, and with finances in good order from new and ongoing productions, the Audubons purchased land by the Hudson River in New York and built a large house. For a time they enjoyed prosperity, as John James continued to take part in expeditions and his sons carried on the family business. Victor and John soon remarried and built houses of their own on the Audubon tract, between them fathering thirteen children. In many respects these may have been satisfying years for Lucy, as she managed a comfortable household, surrounded by her burgeoning family. At long last her husband was justly famous, his productions widely acclaimed. Perhaps she felt her years of hard work and sacrifice had been worth it.

But new sorrows were lurking. John James suffered a debilitating stroke in 1847 and slipped into dementia, dying in 1851. Within a few years Victor had an accident that left him an invalid, unable to help his brother with ongoing projects or management of the family property. The Civil War cut off important Southern subscribers to a new edition of *The Birds of America* that John had undertaken. Overwhelmed and weakened by responsibilities he, too, fell ill. By 1862 both sons were dead, leaving behind substantial debt, the business in ruins. Stunned by their untimely loss and beset with financial woes, Lucy sold her house in 1863. By then she'd already returned to teaching to support herself and assist her struggling family. At 75, Lucy was sharing a boarding house room with a beloved grandchild (Harriette, John's daughter from his first marriage) in an upper Manhattan neighborhood where the younger woman taught music.

Toward the end of my research on this book, as I sorted through a file in the library of The New York Historical Society, two letters slipped from a manila folder. Penned in a shaky hand, they were Lucy's missives to distant relations, mailed not long before her death at 86. The brief decades of stability were over, her husband and sons dead many years. In the Rhodes biography I'd read that Lucy surrendered more than 400 of John James' original drawings for $2000 (about $41,000 today), and sold the engraving plates for scrap when no one would preserve them. I thought about how painful that must have been for her and considered the many millions of dollars others have made from John James' work, as compared to the financial gain it provided him and his family.

Then I reread both letters, still trying to make out Lucy's cramped script. She is infirm now, living once more with Kentucky relatives. Grateful, she writes, for a decent bed. They are short letters, resigned in tone, offering no new information. But I held them in my hands for a long time.

Chronology

Date	Chronology	Historical Context
1785	The product of a shipboard romance, Jean Rabin is born to Jean Audubon and Jeanne Rabin in Les Cayes, Saint-Domingue (present-day Haiti).	John Adams (later the 2nd U.S. president) becomes the first U.S. ambassador to England.
1786	Jeanne Rabin dies. Jean is raised by his father's housekeeper in Les Cayes.	
1787	Lucy Bakewell, the first of six children, is born to William Bakewell and Lucy Green Bakewell at Burton-on-Trent, England.	Delegates arrive in Philadelphia to write a new U.S. constitution. Mozart's opera *Don Giovanni* premieres in Prague.
1791	Young Jean Rabin is sent to France, formally adopted by his father and his father's wife, and his name changed to Jean-Jacques Fougère Audubon.	Mozart's opera *The Magic Flute* debuts in Vienna. Slave revolt overtakes Saint-Domingue. The French Revolution progresses through counterrevolution to "the reign of terror." Thomas Paine's *Rights of Man* is published in London.
1801	The William Bakewell family arrives in America, settles in Connecticut.	Thomas Jefferson becomes the 3rd U.S. president. The first steam powered vehicle transports passengers in Cambourne, England.

1803	Jean-Jacques Audubon arrives in America, settles on a Pennsylvania farm his father bought years earlier, anglicizes his name. William Bakewell buys a plantation in Pennsylvania, relocates his family from Connecticut.	The Louisiana Purchase is negotiated with France, adding 828,000 square miles to U.S. territory. Ohio becomes the 17th state. Beethoven completes his Symphony No. 3, the *Eroica*.
1804	Lucy Bakewell and John James Audubon meet at Fatland Ford. Lucy's mother dies. The following year William Bakewell will marry Rebecca Smith of Philadelphia.	Aaron Burr kills Alexander Hamilton in a politically motivated duel. The Lewis and Clark expedition begins its journey.
1808	Lucy weds John James at Fatland Ford; they depart for Louisville, Kentucky with Ferdinand Rozier, with whom John James will open a general store.	The importation of slaves is banned in the U.S. Ornithologist and illustrator Alexander Wilson publishes *American Ornithology,* Vol.1.
1809	Victor Gifford Audubon is born in Louisville, Kentucky. John James decides to sell his interest in Mill Grove.	Abraham Lincoln is born in Hodgenville, Kentucky. Charles Darwin, grandson of the Bakewells' friend Erasmus Darwin, is born in England.
1810	The Audubon family moves to Henderson, Kentucky, where they again take up storekeeping. John James meets Alexander Wilson, takes him on collecting expeditions, and reviews his drawings, but	The U.S. annexes West Florida from Spain. Chile declares independence from Spain.

cont.	declines to subscribe to his book. This begins a permanent rivalry between the two naturalists.	
1811	Audubon dissolves his partnership with Rozier. Lucy, John James, and Victor travel to Fatland Ford for an extended visit. John James and Tom Bakewell decide to go into business together.	A series of earthquakes begins at New Madrid, Missouri, and lasts for several months.
1812	The Audubons return to Henderson, moving in temporarily with friends, the Rankins, along with Lucy's brother Tom. John Woodhouse Audubon is born.	The War of 1812 begins between the U.S. and England, interfering with trade between the two countries. Napoleon invades Russia.
1813	John James and Tom open and run stores together. The family departs the Rankins' farm for a large, double log home in town.	James Madison, 4th U.S. President, is sworn in for a 2nd term. Jane Austen's *Pride & Prejudice* is published.
1814	John James and Tom travel to explore other business opportunities.	British troops burn Washington, including the Capitol and the president's mansion.
1815	A daughter, also named Lucy, is born in Henderson. Bakewell siblings Eliza and Will join the Audubon household.	The Treaty of Ghent ends the War of 1812.

1816	Lucy's sister Eliza Bakewell marries Nicholas Berthoud. Her brother Tom marries Elizabeth Rankin Page, who persuades him to abandon the businesses and depart to Louisville. The Audubons' baby daughter dies.	James Monroe is elected 5th U.S. president.
1818	Jean Audubon dies in France.	The 49th Parallel forms a border between Canada and the U.S.
1819	The Audubons' continued money problems lead to bankruptcy and the loss of their businesses and home. Another daughter, Rose, is born in Shippingport, Kentucky but dies within the year.	The Panic of 1819 (instigated by the terms of the Louisiana Purchase of 1803) results in widespread financial disruption throughout the U.S.
1820	The Audubons move to Cincinnati, Ohio, where John James has been hired by the Western Museum. When the museum is unable to pay him what they agreed, he and his new assistant, James Mason, depart by flatboat, bound for New Orleans.	Mount Rainier erupts in what is now Washington state.
1821	William Bakewell dies at Fatland Ford. John James and Joseph Mason reach New Orleans. Lucy and sons follow from Shippingport, where they have been staying with Eliza and her family.	The U.S. buys east Florida from Spain. Mexico wins its independence. Napoleon dies on St. Helena. Missouri becomes the 24th state.

1822	Due to the Audubons' financial woes, Lucy takes a position as live-in companion to Anne Brand. John James moves to Natchez, Mississippi with their sons, and continues to collect and paint birds.	Liberia is founded by freed U.S. slaves. An outbreak of yellow fever hits New York. Ulysses S. Grant is born in Point Pleasant, Ohio.
1823	The family moves to Beech Woods plantation, where Lucy has found a position as tutor. Banished in a dispute with the owner, John James returns to Natchez with Victor. Lucy and John later join them.	The Monroe Doctrine establishes U.S. neutrality. The first steamboat navigates the Mississippi River.
1824	The Audubons return to Beech Woods where Lucy resumes teaching. John James instructs neighbors in fencing, drawing and dancing, travels to the Great Lakes and other parts of the eastern U. S., prepares for departure to Europe.	John Ross petitions Congress regarding lands belonging to the Cherokees. The Iowa Tribe is removed to a Kansas reservation.
1826	John James sails for Liverpool, England. Engraver William Lizars agrees to undertake *The Birds of America.*	The American Temperance Society is formed in Boston.
1827	Lucy moves her school to Beech Grove plantation. John James enlists a new engraver, Robert Havell.	The first American railroad company is incorporated. Ludwig van Beethoven dies in Vienna.

1828	Lucy expands her teaching duties at Beech Grove. John James travels in England, Scotland, and France to promote *The Birds of America*.	Gold is discovered in Georgia on Cherokee land.
1829	John James returns to America and reunites with Lucy. Lucy concludes her lessons, bids farewell to her beloved music students and begins packing. John James hunts and gathers specimens for his ongoing work. The couple prepares to depart from Louisiana; they will travel north to visit family and friends before sailing to England in April 1830—there to supervise new plates and promotion for *The Birds of America* subscriptions.	Andrew Jackson becomes the 7th president. Gioachino Rossini's opera *William Tell* premieres in Paris. The typewriter is invented.
1831– 1847	The Audubons return from England, purchase land on the Hudson River and build a house. John James continues his expeditions while his sons run the business with uneven success (due to many factors). Victor and John marry daughters of a family friend, remarry when their wives die early from tuberculosis. John James suffers a stroke and declines into dementia.	Covered wagons transport people from Missouri River towns to settle in California. Florida becomes the 27th state. Hospitals begin to use antiseptics to clean wounds, surgical instruments, and their surgeons' hands. The P.T. Barnum circus tours the U.S.

1851–1863	John James Audubon dies at home in 1851. His business continues a decline, due to the expense of publication, mishaps on expeditions led by his son John, the start of the Civil War, and other problems. Victor dies from complications of an accident, John from overwork and an illness. Lucy returns to teaching, sells her house and her husband's original drawings.	The presidency of the United States passes from Millard Fillmore, through Franklin Pierce and James Buchanan to Abraham Lincoln. Kansas is admitted to the Union in 1861, the 34th state. The Civil War begins.
1874	Lucy dies of pneumonia in Shelbyville, Kentucky, at the home of her brother Will. Granddaughters Harriette and Lucy from John's first marriage escort her remains to New York. She is buried beside her husband in Trinity Cemetery.	The first compulsory education law is passed by New York State. A natural history museum is founded in San Diego, California. Poet Robert Frost is born in San Francisco.

BAKEWELL·AUDUBON

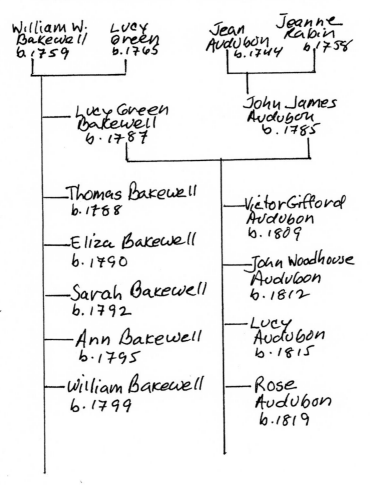

William W. Bakewell b.1759 — Lucy Green b.1765

Jean Audubon b.1744 — Jeanne Rabin b.1758

Lucy Green Bakewell b.1787 — John James Audubon b.1785

Thomas Bakewell b.1788

Eliza Bakewell b.1790

Sarah Bakewell b.1792

Ann Bakewell b.1795

William Bakewell b.1799

Victor Gifford Audubon b.1809

John Woodhouse Audubon b.1812

Lucy Audubon b.1815

Rose Audubon b.1819

Notes

Page xiii: Information about the Audubons contained in the Preface comes from my reading of *John James Audubon: The Making of an American* by Richard Rhodes and *Lucy Audubon: A Biography* by Carolyn E. DeLatte, supplemented by additional reading in John James' published works and collections of his writings edited by others.

Page 11: "Henderson, Kentucky." The italicized lines in this poem are from John James Audubon's *Ornithological Biography, or an Account of the Habits of the Birds of the United States of America*, Volume III, page 122.

Page 13: "A Visit to Fatland Ford." The italicized lines in this poem are found in a letter from Lucy Bakewell to Miss (& Mrs.) Gifford, Lucy's cousin, which is held in the John James Audubon Collection, Manuscripts Division, Department of Rare Books and Special Collections at Princeton University Library.

Page 16: John James Audubon wrote *Ornithological Biography* in three volumes published between 1831 and 1835, a companion to his subscription series of bird prints (which became the book *The Birds of America*). Although the vignettes he often included in the biographies are similar to entries in his journals, they were written later, often long after the events described took place. "Broad-winged Hawk" appears in Volume I of *OB*, pp. 461–462.

Page 17: Earthquakes in the vicinity of New Madrid, Missouri, were the biggest in U.S. history and much commented on at the time. On page 234 of *Audubon and His Journals*, Vol. II, by Maria R. Audubon, John James details his personal encounter with one of the first quakes, late in 1811.

Page 24: Before scientific breakthroughs in the eighteenth and nineteenth centuries brought new ideas and tools to the medical profession, infant mortality rates were shockingly high. It has been estimated that prior to 1900 a third of American children died before their fifth birthdays. On the frontier, this percentage may have been higher. Doctors could provide little more than comfort and symptomatic relief for many diseases and conditions; families dealt with suffering and death as part of daily life.

Page 29: "Passenger Pigeon" appears in Volume I of *Ornithological Biography*, pp. 323–24.

Page 31: In *The Audubon Reader,* page 93, Rhodes discusses the Louisiana Purchase of 1803 and the severe financial trauma caused by final payment of the debt in 1819. The Audubons were among the many business owners negatively affected. In *Lucy Audubon: A Biography*, page 93, DeLatte writes that the Henderson bank was one of the first to fail in what became known as the Panic of 1819—a general collapse of the economy that persisted for several years.

Page 33: "Partial Bill of Sale" is based, in part, on an inventory prepared by John James for the sale of the family's possessions, as detailed in *The Audubon Reader* by Richard Rhodes, pp. 93–94.

Page 50: "*Fair Incognito.*" The letter from which the italicized lines are taken, "Audubon Journal May 31, 1821," is part of the John James Audubon Papers, 1821–1845, held at the American Philosophical Library.

Page 56: On page 211 of *John James Audubon: The Making of an American,* Richard Rhodes describes Matabon as "an old friend from Louisville, an elderly professional flutist" who was "ragged, broke and hungry" when Audubon found him in the marketplace and invited him home. The Audubons often hosted visitors for extended periods, as was common in a time when hotels tended to be scarce, vermin-infested, expensive, and uncomfortable.

Page 60: Yellow-toned skin might imply either health issues resulting from a disease or a mixed-race ancestry.

Page 61: This incident highlights Lucy's domestic servant status in the Percy household. To a woman born into English gentry and until recently the owner of considerable property herself (including several slaves), this intimate intrusion must have been mortifying, as was likely Jane Percy's intention.

Page 72: "Mocking Bird" appears in Volume I of *Ornithological Biography,* pp. 112–113.

Page 75: Audubon soon became dissatisfied with the quality of work from the Lizars operation. He transferred production to Robert Havell, who completed the plates for *The Birds of America.*

Page 76: Audubon was known to enjoy playing the role of rustic woodsman during his time in England, dressing in skins and smearing his long hair with grease. Audubon was always a bit of a dandy, proud of his appearance, so this was most likely a marketing ploy and evidently successful.

Page 79: John James regularly addressed his wife in his journals, often quoting from these entries in later correspondence with her.

Page 81: These letter fragments, taken from the Richard Rhodes compilation of Audubon writings *The Audubon Reader,* pp. 213 and 217, underscore the difficulty of carrying on a relationship via unreliable transatlantic mail service. Letters could be delayed for many months or never arrive at all. Answers, explanations, and rejoinders might cross en route, further inflaming misunderstandings. Duplicate letters were sometimes sent via different ships, to increase the chance of being received in a timely manner.

Page 96: The italicized lines are from "Letter to Lucy Audubon, May 6, 1829," part of the John James Audubon Papers, 1821–1845, which are held at the American Philosophical Library.

Page 97: The italicized lines are from *Letters of John James Audubon 1826–1840*, by John James Audubon, page 80.

Page 103: As with the Preface, the Afterword draws its information from my reading of *John James Audubon: The Making of an American* by Richard Rhodes and *Lucy Audubon: A Biography* by Carolyn E. DeLatte.

Works Cited and Consulted

Alexander, Pamela. *Commonwealth of Wings: An Ornithological Biography Based on the Life of John James Audubon*, Wesleyan UP, 1991.

Audubon, John James. *Audubon and His Journals*, edited by Maria R. Audubon, Vol. I & II, Scribner's, 1897.

Audubon, John James. *John James Audubon Writings & Drawings*, edited by Christoph Irmscher, The Library of America, 1999.

Audubon, John James. *Journal of John James Audubon: Made During His Trip to New Orleans in 1820–21*, edited by Howard Corning, The Club of Odd Volumes, 1929.

Audubon, John James. *Letters of John James Audubon, 1826–1840*, edited by Howard Corning, The Club of Odd Volumes, 1930.

Audubon, John James. "Letter to Lucy Audubon, May 6, 1829." *John James Audubon Papers, 1821–1845*. American Philosophical Society Library.

Audubon, John James. "Letter to Lucy Audubon, May 31, 1821." *John James Audubon Papers, 1821–1845*. American Philosophical Society Library.

Audubon, John James. *Ornithological Biography, or an Account of the Habits of the Birds of The United States of America*, Vol I, II & III, Edinburgh, 1831, 1834 & 1835.

Audubon, John James. *The Audubon Reader*, edited by Richard Rhodes, Knopf, 2006.

Audubon, John James. *The Life of John James Audubon, the Naturalist*, edited by Lucy Green Bakewell Audubon, Putnam, 1869.

Audubon, Lucy Bakewell. "Letter to Miss (& Mrs.) Gifford," John James Audubon Collection, Manuscripts Division, Department of Rare Books and Special Collections, Princeton University Library.

DeLatte, Carolyn E. *Lucy Audubon: A Biography*, Louisiana State UP, 2008.

Mozart, Wolfgang Amadeus. *The Magic Flute* (1791), Libretto by Emanuel Schikaneder, Schirmer, 1941.

Nooteboom, Cees. *The Following Story*. Translated by Ina Rilke, Random House, 2014.

Rhodes, Richard. *John James Audubon: The Making of an American*, Knopf, 2004.

Welty, Eudora. "A Silent Moment." *The Wide Net and Other Stories*, Harcourt Brace, 1943.

Image Credits

The following five images (all in the public domain) are from John James Audubon's book *The Birds of America.* They are reproduced courtesy of the John James Audubon Center at Mill Grove in Audubon, Pennsylvania and the Montgomery County, Pennsylvania Audubon collection:

Page 15: Broad-winged Hawk, Plate 91

Page 25: American Sparrow Hawk, Plate 142

Page 48: Downy Woodpecker, Plate 112

Page 62: Swamp Sparrow, Plate 64

Page 71: Mocking Bird, Plate 21

Page 78: Portrait of John James Audubon 1826, by John Syme, from the White House collection, Washington, D.C., and in the public domain.

Page 89: Unknown Photographer after a miniature of Lucy Bakewell Audubon from ca. 1831 by Frederick Cruikshank (1880–1868), Photograph from a copy negative, Department of Prints, Photographs, and Architectural Collections, New York Historical Society.

Acknowledgments

To the editors of journals and anthologies where these poems first appeared, some in earlier form, my appreciation:

"Light" and "Almost Morning": *Schuylkill Valley Journal*
"Audubon, Distracted": *US1 Worksheets*
"Dear Eliza": *Forgotten Women* (Grayson Books, 2017)

Versions of "Audubon, Abroad" and "Dear Eliza" were also included in my collection *Mango in Winter* (Grayson Books, 2013).

Without Rose Metal's superb editors, Kathleen Rooney and Abigail Beckel, this would be a different book. Their ideas and guidance much improved the manuscript and helped me realize my fondest dreams for it. To both of them, my boundless thanks.

I am deeply grateful to everyone else who advised me—from the book's inception as a few poems about John James Audubon, through years of a changing and expanded project—in particular, Barbara Daniels and Lois Marie Harrod, who generously undertook close readings and provided invaluable insight at several critical points. Fellow members of the performance ensemble Cool Women—Eloise Bruce, Betty Lies, Lois Harrod, Judy Michaels, Sharon Olson, Penelope Schott, Maxine Susman, and Gretna Wilkinson—contributed information and ongoing encouragement, as did members of the US1 Poets Cooperative. My thanks to all of them and to the many others who offered their ideas and enthusiasm.

Especially, and always, I am indebted to my husband James for his interest, patience, love, and steadfast support.

About the Author

Juditha Dowd is the author of a full-length poetry collection, *Mango in Winter* (Grayson Books, 2013), as well as short fiction, lyric essays, and three poetry chapbooks—*The Weathermancer* (Finishing Line, 2006), *What Remains* (Finishing Line, 2009), and *Back Where We Belong* (Casa de Cinco Hermanas, 2012). Her work appears in many journals and anthologies, including *Poet Lore, Poetry Daily, Verse Daily, The Florida Review, Spillway, Rock & Sling, Kestrel,* and *About Place.* With the ensemble Cool Women she regularly performs poetry in the New York-Philadelphia metro area and occasionally on the west coast. Juditha currently lives in Easton, Pennsylvania with her husband and two cats, not far from where Lucy Bakewell began her long-ago adventure with John James Audubon. Visit her website at www.judithadowd.org.

A Note About the Type

The events in *Audubon's Sparrow* are set in the early 1800s, so the fonts were chosen to evoke the historical context while also maintaining a subtle modern sensibility to match the hybrid collaged form of Juditha Dowd's biography of Lucy Bakewell Audubon.

The text and titles are set in Crimson Text, an open-source typeface designed by Sebastian Kosch and released via Google Fonts in 2010. It's an old-style serif inspired by classics like Garamond that has a sturdy and practical sensibility—rather than the fanciful flourishes that are typical of old-style calligraphic fonts—that feels appropriate to Lucy's personality and life.

The front cover features the font Broadsheet. It was designed by Brian Willson in 2006 and released by Three Islands Press, a foundry that specializes in fonts modeled after antique penmanship. Broadsheet's design was inspired by the type on printed materials published in Colonial America, notably issues of *The New-England Weekly Journal* from 1728 and the *Massachusetts Sun* from 1775.

—Heather Butterfield